T0380843

A BOY BECOMES A MAN

You Can Do It!

by

Julian Lorenzana

Illustrated by Kersly Minoza

ISBN: Softcover 978-1-4990-4174-3
EBook 978-1-4990-4173-6

Illustrations on pages 8, 10, 19, 30, 32, 35 and 50 by Glenna Smith.

Rev. date: 08/28/2014

To order additional copies of this book, contact:
Xlibris LLC
1-888-795-4274
www.Xlibris.com
Orders@Xlibris.com

DEDICATION

I dedicate this book to the love of my life, my wife, Teresa, who has been suffering with Parkinson's Disease for the last 32 years. This terrible disease has taken away her ability to think, to see to hear and to speak. But, while all her senses were intact, she did all she could to encourage me in my most important endeavors and hobbies, including my singing, my song writing and my story writing. Even now, during her moments of lucidity, she sometimes asks me, "How is your story coming along?" And when I answer with "You will see the results soon," she will simply give me a big smile.

May God reward her in some positive way for her suffering and for all the encouragement she has given me.

TABLE OF CONTENTS

Chapter 1 | A Death in the Family 7

Chapter 2 | Julio, the Goat Herder 16

Chapter 3 | Treed by a Mountain Lion 22

Chapter 4 | Julio Tries Pig Herding 28

Chapter 5 | Julio Wants His Goats Back 40

Chapter 6 | Julio Decides to Stick with Pig Herding 47

Chapter 7 | Julio Says Good-bye 55

CHAPTER 1

A DEATH IN THE FAMILY

"Please, God, help me! Please, God, help me!" I could hear myself pleading between sobs as I lay up on a tree. Terror wouldn't allow me the sleep I so desperately needed. All I could do was relive the events of the past few years. Doing well in school had been my only challenge and I always managed it but that fantasy world, a world free of cares and full of happy dreams, came to an abrupt halt when I was seven years old.

One spring morning, Mother picked my two big sisters and me up at school and gave us some bad news. "All three of you are getting big," she said, her voice soft and soothing. "That is why I feel I can give you the bad news I bring. Your daddy has just passed away and you have to come home."

Though she tried to hide it, I sensed her grief. Her voice cracked into sobs that shook my whole body. I wanted to cry but I held back my tears. How I held my emotions in check at that moment, I will never know. I had always been accustomed to giving free rein to my feelings. My sisters couldn't hold back their tears.

"Please, don't worry about it, mother. We'll make out all right," I told her, even though, deep inside, I knew that we would miss him terribly. My father's death was a big blow to everyone, especially to me.

From the day he died, I kept thinking about the day when I would have to quit school in order to go to work to help support the family.

My days in school went by slowly, happy most of the time, except when I thought of my father. Those days were very sad for me because I thought of those happy days when I played and sang with him. I do not recall too many times when he and I interacted but those incidents I do remember bring me great joy and sadness at the same time.

We were extremely poor and, even though he was a very hard worker, he could not afford to buy us the kinds of toys other children played with. I remember one time when he found some soda bottle caps and told me, "Julio, this is going to be your new toy. I'll have it ready for you by tomorrow."

"How is that going to be a toy?" I asked him. "To me, it is simply a bottle cap," I added.

"You'll see, son. You will have something to play with," he assured me.

Two days later, after supper, he gave me my new toy. One of the bottle caps had been hammered flat. Two holes had been drilled through the middle and a two foot string had been strung through the holes and tied at the ends. He saw my puzzled face so he said, "I will show you how to use it tomorrow. It is called a zumbador."

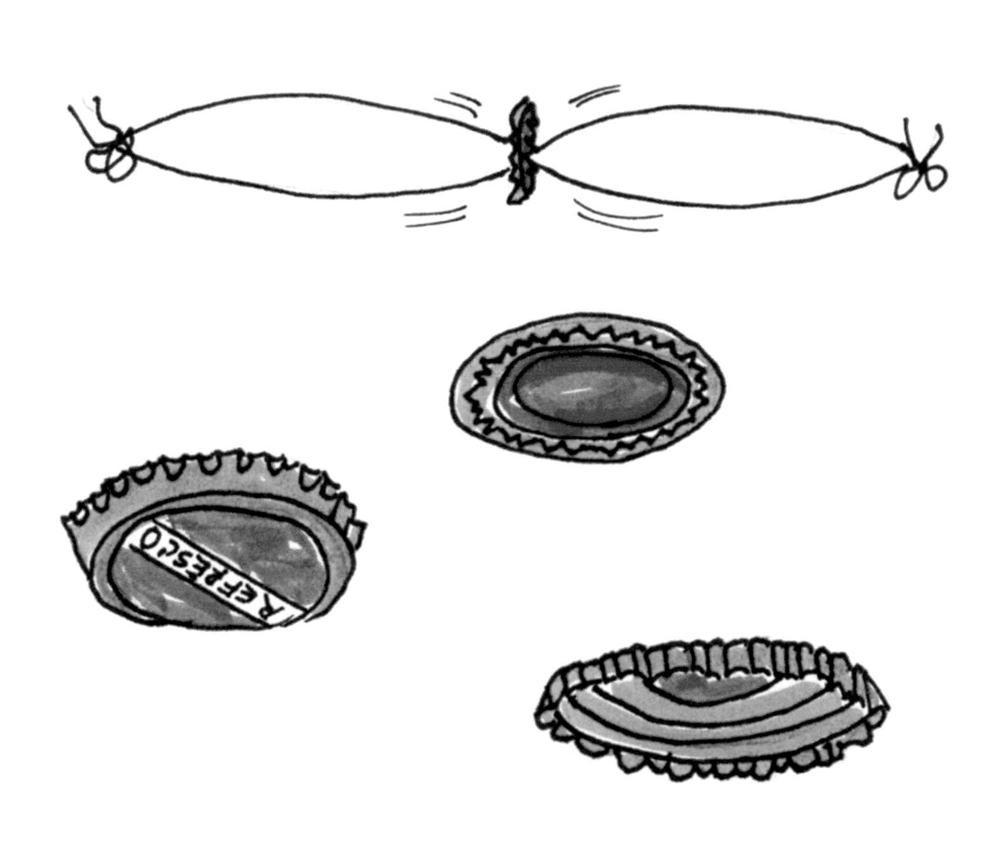
REFRESCO

Then, the whole family went outside, as was usual when he had nothing special to do. He set up some things to sit on: a flat rock, a chair, a box, a bench. Once we were all sitting down, he would ask, "What do you want to sing?"

Whoever thought of a song first would raise his or her hand and blurt out the name of the tune. If we all knew it, Dad would start singing and we would follow along. I remember three or four of us would sing along with him. Once we were all on pitch, he or Eva would sing the harmony part. After each song, he would say, "You are all doing great. I'm sure some day at least one of you will become a professional singer. I'm really proud of you." Then, he would ask my mother, "Don't you agree, Chuy?"

My mother would simply answer, "I don't sing but you sounded real good."

After we sang about five or six songs, he would tell us, "It's late already. Let's go to bed. Some of us have to get up early tomorrow."

He must have been paying special attention to my singing because, before we went to bed, he said, "We're looking for someone to take over Joselito's place in our Pastorela group. He is the little boy who sings the lullaby to baby Jesus with María. His whole family has moved away and we need a replacement. I really think you are ready to take his place, Julio. I know you are only six years old but your singing has improved a lot. Would you like to take Joselito's place? I have heard you singing that lullaby so many times, I think you must know it already. All you have to do is rehearse it with María a few times and you will do a great job. Will you do it?"

"If you think I am ready and the other members of the Pastorela agree, I will do it," I said. "As long as you help me learn it completely, I'm sure I'll be ready. I just hope I can control my nerves on the days of the performances," I added.

"Okay. That's settled. You will be fine. Now let's go to sleep," he said.

Another of my fond memories is one where he was putting a roof on our new house. We had been living in a thatched roof house, of which I cannot remember anything. The walls on our new house were made of adobe and he was now putting red, Spanish tiles on the roof. I was playing with my new zumbador on top of the piles of adobes he had made for the house.

The rainy season was approaching and he was in a hurry to finish the roof. The sky became very cloudy. He had barely completed half of the roof in one room when, suddenly, the rain started, at first lightly and then heavily. We ran to the sheltered part of the room. My mother pleaded with him to get down out of the rain but he kept on working. Fortunately, the rain stopped as suddenly as it had begun. The sun came up and we resumed the activities we were engaged in before the rain had come.

My mother tried to convince him to get down while it was raining and after it had stopped but he kept on working. He was all wet and she was worried about him getting sick and she urged him to get down to at least change his clothes.

"Sweetheart, you are soaking wet and it's a little cold. You're going to get sick. Come down and change into dry clothes. Then you can continue working. The Pastorela is this coming Sunday. If you're sick, you won't be able to sing. Come down and change clothes," she begged him.

"I can't, Chuy," he said. "See those clouds in the distance? They will probably be here in two or three hours. I have to finish roofing at least this room. I'll be okay. I'm not cold at all," he insisted. Fortunately, he was able to finish the roof before the rain fell again.

Sunday came and, in preparation for Christmas, we put on the Pastorela for the first time. My father was not sick. I learned my part as well as I could and the performance went on very smoothly.

I can say it was a huge success because applause and congratulations were abundant. My part in the group became permanent, as my father told me, "Son, you did a great job! Of course, I always knew you could do it. Congratulations!"

"Thank you, dad. Without your help I would not have been able to do it," I said.

Singing in the Pastorela turned out to be a very enjoyable, as well as valuable, experience. It was enjoyable because it allowed me to spend more time with my dad. We went to all the Pastorela rehearsals together. Sometimes he would sing Maria's part in a duet with me. It felt great!

Years later, after he was gone, nearby haciendas or towns would invite us to perform the Pastorela and we would oblige. These performances were valuable for voice development reasons but mainly because, as payment, we were given a typically Mexican meal. As was mentioned before, we were quite poor and couldn't afford special meals. I would eat so much I would end up with a very uncomfortable stomach and even vomit, sometimes. I remained on the Pastorela until we moved out of my home town four years later.

Though these happy memories bring me great sadness, I enjoy replaying them in my mind. But, like any other child, I was able to forget the sad things and concentrate on my studies. My days in school were full of friendships and fun activities. The second big blow to my world, that world free of cares and full of happy dreams, came when I was ten.

CHAPTER 2

JULIO, THE GOAT HERDER

One day before the school year was to begin, my two younger siblings were eagerly talking about and preparing themselves for school when my mother took me aside and told me, "Julio, you are already ten years old. I think you are old enough to help us with the support of the family. I don't like the idea of taking you out of school, seeing how much you like it. But I will have to do it. Mr. Pedro León is looking for someone to take care of his goats. I'll talk to him about giving you the job. Is that okay?"

"I guess so. But I don't know anything about goat herding or herding anything!" I answered.

"You will learn on the job after Mr. León gives you some instructions. Don't worry. You're a fast learner. Besides, we still don't know if he will give you the job," she told me.

I was kind of apprehensive about any kind of job. Not only was I totally unprepared for any kind of job but I was also a cowardly child. The only place I had ever gone by myself was to school and that didn't take much bravery.

“Will I be able to do the job if I get hired?” I asked my mother and myself repeatedly. Visions of mountain lions eating me and the goats danced in my head. Mother assured me, “Everything will be all right. Your goat herding would not take you to places where wild animals are found.” Two days later, I found out that Mr. León had hired me, despite my lack of preparation.

A creek that comes down from the mountains nearby forks into two creeks as it hits our town. One creek runs south while the other one runs west, thus cutting our town into three parts. During the rainy season, this creek creates havoc on the villagers by flooding the houses situated between the two parts of the creek. But the rainy season was still months away so I didn't have to worry about it.

Our grazing plains were separated from those mountains by a low fence. “Try to keep the herd away from the fence at all times,” Mr. León warned me as I set out on my first herding assignment. “Mountain lions have been known to come down as far as the fence. I'm afraid to think of what would happen if the goats find a hole in that fence,” his words rang loudly in my ears the closer the herd got to the fence. I got to my chosen grazing area without any of my goats wandering away from the herd and they grazed calmly for hours.

A few hours before sunset, I rounded them up and began the trip home. Though my body was somewhat tired, my heart swelled with pride. “Thank you, Lord, for helping me through the day. I think my goats and I will be all right,” I whispered as we started for home. Singing has always been a pastime of mine so I began to sing a tune to the rhythm of my steps.

"Come on, my herd,
Join me in my singing
I think I heard
The church bells ringing

We're almost there
I hear some talking
Time let's not spare
Let's keep on walking

Hurray for us
We'll soon be resting
That's why........

I stopped singing suddenly because I spotted a man and his dog in the distance walking toward us. As they came closer, his dog began to bark at the herd. The man tried hard to calm his dog but he failed. Frightened, the goats began to run away in all directions. Soon, they all headed straight to the fence. To make matters worse, they found a break in it and they disappeared from sight.

"Look what your dog has done!" I screamed with anger. "Why didn't you hold him back? What am I going to do now?" I asked.

"I'm terribly sorry. I tried to hold him back but I couldn't," he apologized. "Listen, I can help you round them up if you want me to," he added.

"Go away and leave me alone! Take that stupid dog with you! I don't need your help!" I blurted out, not realizing what I was saying. My head was spinning. Common sense had deserted me. By the time I calmed down, the man and his dog had disappeared.

Fear and anger swelled within me again as I realized that I was in deep trouble. I thought, "If I had not let my emotions run away from me, I would not be in this predicament. I should have let him help me round them up. But no! I let anger rule the moment!"

For a while, I stood there bewildered, not knowing what to do while the entire herd disappeared. When my anger and my fear subsided, I began to climb up the mountain in search of my goats. This search continued for hours without success. When the sun set, my fears multiplied as I realized that soon, darkness would cover the area and my job would become even more difficult. I decided to speed up my search before total darkness arrived.

My search soon took me to a small creek whose clear, sparkling water offered me relief from the terrible thirst I had begun to feel. As I drank, a thought crossed my mind. "If I am thirsty, the goats must be thirsty, too. I am sure they are somewhere near this creek."

For miles I walked up along the creek but I didn't see any of my goats. As darkness began to fall upon the area, fear, hunger, cold and hopelessness gripped my heart. Fear now more for myself than for my goats.

After what seemed like a very long time, I came to the source of the creek. By this time, I was hungry but the only thing left in my lunch sack was a chocolate bar and a little box of matches. I built a small fire near the spring, sat down and munched on the chocolate while the sounds of frogs, owls and crickets kept me company.

How alone I felt in that darkness, despite the noisy company! After eating, I decided to follow the creek downward, hoping to run into my herd. I thought this creek ran through my village and I hoped it would lead me back home.

Moments later, I heard growls of what I thought was a mountain lion. At first, I was not worried as they sounded too far away. Soon, though, the growls became louder and I quickened my pace as my heart began to pound faster and faster. I found a few goats resting by the creek and happiness began to take hold of my heart.

Soon, I found what I hoped was the rest of my goats. My fear could not completely disappear, though, because growls could still be heard along our route once in a while. Each growl sounded closer and closer. "Could some mountain lion be preying on us?" I asked myself fearfully. To drive away that fear, I began to talk to the goats. "We do not want to become a banquet for some hungry lion, do we? Soon, you will be safe in your pen and I will be safe at home with my family. Come on, let's hurry it up!"

CHAPTER 3

TREED BY A MOUNTAIN LION

Suddenly, a terrifying, drawn-out growl pierced the silence of the night! It froze me momentarily! I tried hard to collect my thoughts but the pounding of my heart made it quite difficult to do so! "God almighty, please protect us! What should I do?" These words I uttered without thinking. Perhaps my religious upbringing came to the fore in that instant of need. A tree I had not noticed before because of my fear, suddenly came into view and I quickly climbed up to a safe height. All thought of the herd and its safety had left me. At that moment, I thought only of my own safety. I clung to a tree branch for hours, shivering with fear and cold.

In the wee hours of the morning, my wits returned. I thought of staying up on the tree until someone would come to my rescue but I soon realized that it would probably take hours before any one would find me.

What a sight! Me up a tree hugging a branch! I thought and prayed for a way out of my predicament but fear did not allow me to think clearly. I knew dawn would come soon and the surrounding area would become more visible. I could still hear growls in the distance but I couldn't see anything.

As I leaned forward to strengthen my grip on the branch, I felt something in my shirt pocket. "Matches, matches!" I screamed excitedly. "Big cats stay away from bonfires in the movies. Maybe it's true in real life," I thought. "I'll have to check it out. There is plenty of firewood around. Not only will the fire keep wild animals away. People may see it and it will lead them to me," I added hopefully.

A chilling thought crowded my clear thinking momentarily. "What if a mountain lion suddenly swoops down upon me while I'm building the fire?" But that thought was quickly replaced by a more encouraging one. "I can always climb up the tree right away. I'll just stay as close to the tree as possible."

Before I could lose my confidence, I climbed down and rounded up as much wood as I could. My eyes and ears were kept wide open for any approaching danger. Fortunately, my bonfire was set without any problems. I climbed up the tree and stayed there for as long as possible. I got down once in a while only to add wood to the fire.

I stayed up the tree for what seemed like an eternity. While up on the tree, I looked around hoping to see any of my goats or any people looking for me. But it was impossible to distinguish anything in that dark environment. Beyond a few yards, blackness was all I could see.

After getting down several times to add wood to the fire, I decided to stay up until dawn appeared. Time seemed to move at a snail's pace. What I thought were hours passing by were merely minutes. I was so upset with the speed of the time going by that I went crazy. I started rambling something to God. "Please, God, make the time go by faster! I'm getting really tired and sleepy. You know very well I can't relax because you know what will happen as soon as I fall asleep. I will stop hugging this beautiful branch and it will get mad at me. It will let me go and I will go tumbling down to a fateful thud on the ground. If I don't kill myself, I will break my bones. And disabled, any wild animal will make a meal out of me. You don't want that for me, do you? Besides, I'm too young to die. Please help me. I know you can make the hours pass by in a second. Please, God, have pity on me," I pleaded.

When I realized I was pleading with God for help, I felt a little better. My sleepiness did not go away, and I decided I couldn't go to sleep, for obvious reasons.

Instead, I decided to start singing at the top of my voice or count up to one thousand. Once I ran out of songs to sing and my throat was tired and hoarse, I stopped. Fortunately, the first light of dawn had made its appearance and my confidence returned. I had a feeling I would be all right. I realized that my ramblings before the singing were really prayers to God. Somehow I knew He wouldn't let me down. I thanked Him for keeping me awake.

As soon as the sun was about a quarter of the way up in the sky, I heard some men calling my name. My heart began to beat to a different rhythm. Confidence, happiness and gratitude had taken a different grip on it. I began to cry out for help, thinking that someone would hear me.

Soon, I was happy to see two men coming. As they got closer, I recognized them as two of Mr. León's workers, Ramón and Patricio. "Hey, Ramón, here I am, up on the tree!" I yelled.

"We know, Julio! We saw you after we heard you crying for help," answered Patricio.

"Hey, Julio, what are you doing up on that tree? Are you taking in the sights?" Ramón asked jokingly.

"What's the matter? Did you get stuck up there?" Patricio asked. "Come on, we'll help you down. You must be awfully tired up there," he added.

Once I was down, I said, "Boy, you don't know how happy I am to see you! There was a time when I thought I would never get home. Thanks a lot for finding me," I said gratefully. "But how did you know where to find me?" I asked.

"We didn't," Ramón answered. "When your mother showed up at Mr. León's house wanting to know where you were, she seemed really worried. She begged Mr. León to send somebody to look for you. Of course, he had already given us each a rifle and told us to be ready to go out looking for you. And when darkness fell and you hadn't shown up, he really panicked. He was worried more for you than for his herd. That was when we came out looking for you."

"When we first set out, we walked for hours and we almost gave up," said Patricio. "We were kind of spooked because we heard mountain lion growls in the distance. But we kept on and I'm glad we did," he added.

"But why were you up there? Did you spend the whole night up there?" Ramón asked.

"Yes, I did," I answered. "Those growls you said you heard on your way up, I heard them earlier. At first, they sounded too far away. But when they sounded too close, I didn't know what to do. The only thing I could think of was to climb up the tree. I spent the whole night up there thinking, praying, singing and yelling. I did come down once in a while to make and keep up a fire. I thought it would keep animals away," I added.

Now that I felt safe, I remembered my goats. "Did you see any of my goats on your way up the mountain?' I asked them.

Neither of them answered my question right away. They simply looked at me and a terrible thought occurred to me.

"Oh, my God, the mountain lion must have eaten all of them!" I screamed.

After a few minutes of silence, Ramón stared at me and said, "Some adventure you must have had! But don't worry. Everything is under control. Let's go home."

When he said that, I cried not only for joy but also because I had considered myself a failure in my first attempt at being a man.

Back home with my family, everyone made a big fuss over me. Mother cried as she hugged me and said, "I am so happy you are home safe, son! Don't worry about anything. The herd has been found, minus only two goats. Mr. León has found out the real cause of the entire incident and he assured me that the job is still yours." "Thank God!" I said as my mother hugged me and kissed me.

CHAPTER 4

JULIO TRIES PIG HERDING

God must have heard me thanking Him because my job went on fairly smoothly for a few months. But one morning, Mr. León took me aside and asked me, "Julio, tell me how you feel about your job."

"It's all right, I guess. The goats don't stand still for very long. They keep walking constantly. My God! They get me so tired!" I replied.

"Well," said Mr. León. "You are doing fine but I want you to change jobs. How would you like to take care of my pigs? They are slow walkers and they tend to get tired easily, especially during the hottest part of the day. They will find a shady tree and just sit there for hours. That would give you a chance to rest. Do you want to try it? If you don't like it, you can go back to herding goats. Manuel is the regular pig herder but he said he is willing to switch jobs, at least for a while."

"Am I doing something wrong with the goats? How come you want to take them away from me?" I asked him.

"No, no, no, no! You're doing fine," he stated. "I just think I am working you too hard. You are a little boy doing a man's job. You need more rest time and I'm sure the pigs will give it to you. How about it? You can start tomorrow. Talk to your mom about it. I think she will be relieved to know that you won't be walking too much," he said.

"Okay, Mr. León. See you tomorrow," I said.

At sunup the next morning, armed with a sling and a long stick, I showed up at Mr. Leon's ranch-style house to pick up the pigs and to get his last-minute instructions. We counted the pigs. There were thirty in all: eight females, four mean-looking males and eighteen piglets of all sizes. I herded them out of their pen and toward the road. The males led the way, followed by the females and trailing were the piglets. Sure enough, the pace was very slow but noisy, due to the playfulness of the young ones.

We soon hit some fields where the corn crop had been recently harvested and the pigs seemed to enjoy themselves digging up the kernels of corn with their snouts and gobbling them up. They covered a fairly large area of the cornfield but always stayed close together.

When the sun was right above us, the herd began to get excited. Some began to squeal and grunt excitedly. I thought they wanted to fight among themselves and I began to worry. The males did start to get after each other and, to stop them, I began to scream at them.

"What's the matter with you guys? Cut it out! Get away from each other!" One male lunged at another one as if it wanted to eat its ears. As it went after its neck, I decided to do something besides screaming at it. I whacked its behind with my long stick. It squealed, turned around and took after me. It really scared me but the chase was short because, somehow, I was able to climb up the nearest tree.

It stopped and looked at me as I said, "Sorry fellow, but you asked for it. I had to do something before you hurt somebody. You understand, don't you? I'm going to get down now. You won't chase me anymore, will you?" I did not climb down until I saw it turning around to join the other pigs. I wasn't going to trust it while it was facing me. When I finally got down and went toward the herd, the pigs were as calm as they could be. Thank God!

I think the heat was getting to them and the only thing they could do to relieve their bad temper was to go after each other. I spotted a huge, shady tree in the distance and started herding them toward it. Soon, they all lay down on the ground and some were even dozing off.

(7)

They allowed me to sit down and eat my lunch. I made sure I sat down where they wouldn't bother me. Pigs usually want to share what you're eating but they must have been full and tired because they didn't bother me while I ate. We stayed under the tree for a long time. As soon as the rays of the sun became less hot, the herd began to stir. Before we started on our way home, I decided to have a one-sided conversation with them.

"Okay, all of you. We are ready to go home. But before we start, I want to thank you for being a good bunch. Well, all except one of you who tried to get even with me for whacking you. Of course, as soon as you realized you had asked for it, you stopped chasing me. Thank you, fellow. I don't expect any problems on the way back because I know you all will be on your best behavior, right?"

They were quiet while I was talking to them but when my speech was over, they started making all kinds of squeals. I took their squeals as a "yes".

The rainy season was in full swing so I begged them, "Don't wander off. Stay on the road home and hurry. We don't want a storm to drench us. Sure, I have my raincoat but the rain may cause some problems with the tiniest members of our herd. Be good to me, okay?"

We proceeded at a slow pace toward the village. After walking a few kilometers, the herd stopped. The males began to snort strangely and the young ones started squealing, all staring at something in the distance. I got to the front of the herd to investigate. Far in the distance, I could see what appeared to be a large dog walking toward us. To drive their fears away, I began talking to them.

"Hey, don't be afraid. It's only a dog. It won't hurt you. Its owner is probably in the bushes on the side of the road. It will be okay. Let's go on before those black clouds drop their moisture on us." The pigs kept up their squealing and snorting. They seemed to be ready to run away in the direction we had started. I began to make a lot of noise myself. I sang some songs as loudly as I could and shouted at the top of my lungs as I walked toward the intruder. "Hey, whatever you are, get out of the road! You're blocking our path!" As I got closer, I realized it wasn't a dog at all. It was a huge coyote.

I knew it would not eat the whole herd but I was bound to lose at least one. I swung my sling and flung a rock at it. I didn't think I would hit it but I did. As the rock hit it, it yelped in pain and started running away out of sight. I was so proud of myself I yelled, "Yippee! Thank you, God! Now, please keep it away from us and get us home safely."

When I turned around toward the herd, no pig was in sight. All kinds of bad thoughts crept into my head and I blurted out loud, "Oh, God, what if there are more coyotes and the one I chased away was just a decoy used to get me away from the herd! They probably ate all the pigs! Oh, no! Please, God, don't let it be true!"

As I calmed down a little, I realized that I was probably overreacting. Then I thought, "But where are they?" As I got closer, I began to hear their movement, their squealing and their snorting. I found them lying under a tree by the side of the road and I squealed with happiness.

"Hey, fellows, I'm so glad you're still here! I'm sorry I left you all alone for a while but I had to try to shoo that coyote away. You understand, don't you? Now, let me make sure you are all here. Yeah, all thirty of you are here. Now, let's go home. I hope I scared that coyote enough to stay away from us. Keep your eyes open just in case he comes back."

The clouds in the sky were getting darker and darker by the minute and bolts of lighting and roars of thunder got my pigs and me quite nervous. Luckily, the big storm didn't start until the pigs were in their pen. My raincoat kept me from getting too wet on my way home.

Needless to say, my mother was quite happy to see me home. "Julio!" she shouted as I got to my house. "How was your day, son?" she asked. "I hope you didn't have any problems. You look tired. Come in and sit down. I will give you a cup of hot tea to warm you up," she added.

"I'm okay, mom," I assured her. "I'm just tired and a little cold. Nothing interesting happened. I had a few problems but God was with us all the time. I'll tell you about them after I rest for a while. She spread a blanket on the floor and I lay down on it.

My brother and sisters had been listening to our conversation and they were anxious to hear whatever happened to me and the pigs. They didn't believe my day had gone by without anything interesting happening. As I lay on the blanket, they gathered around me and begged me to tell them everything about my day.

"Okay, okay! But I don't know if I will be able to stay awake during my narration. I'm too tired and sleepy," I told them. "Ahaaa!" I yawned. "Well, on our way back, ahaaa . . . . the herd . . . suddenly stopped and I . . . . went to the front to . . . investigate. Please, let me sleep. I'll . . . finish my story . . . tomorrow. I'm . . . I'm . . . I'm too sleepy."

Faking a snore, I closed my eyes and pretended to be asleep. I heard my brother say, "Come on! Finish it now! Julio, Julio, wake up!" My mother helped me as she told them, "Leave him alone! Can't you see he's asleep? Get away from him! Let him sleep!"

I was smiling on the inside because I knew how anxious my siblings were to keep me awake. But I was really tired and I don't even know how soon after I fell asleep. When I woke up from my nap, I was forced to tell my brother and sisters everything. I couldn't escape it. I told them everything, plus a few made up things that never happened. They had waited almost two hours for me to wake up so I felt obligated to spice up my story. I don't know if they believed everything but they seemed happy.

CHAPTER 5

JULIO WANTS HIS GOATS BACK

The weeks rolled by without any outstanding events in my everyday activities. In order to put some pop into my life, I got together with Manuel Díaz, who had taken over herding my goats, to discuss our jobs. We had known each other since our days in school. He was two years older than I was.

"Hey, Manuel, how is your job coming along? Do you like herding goats? Have you had any scary adventures like the one I had a year ago? You know, the time when a mountain lion made me spend the whole night up on a tree."

"Yeah, I like my job and no, nothing scary has happened to me," he answered. "I do remember that day. Everybody was worrying about you. We thought something real bad had happened to you when you failed to return with your herd that night. Did it really happen? Some of us thought you had made it up," he added.

"Hey, I did get the scare of my life! I wouldn't have stayed away from home for so long if I had not been forced to spend the whole night up on a tree. Maybe the mountain lion wasn't as close as I thought it was but I wasn't going to take any chances. Anyway, that was a long time ago. Let's talk about today, okay?"

"Okay. What do you want to talk about? You and I should be switching jobs again. Would you do it?" he asked.

"Hey, that's a great idea! How did you know what I wanted to talk to you about?" I asked.

"I didn't," he answered. "It just occurred to me right now. The fact is I haven't had anything exciting happen to me. Not that I want to get scared out of my pants by a mountain lion like you were. But I wouldn't mind getting my job back. Do you think we can do it? Will Mr. León allow it?" he wondered.

"You leave that to me. I'll talk to him about it. I'm almost sure he will. Even if he doesn't, nothing will be lost," I said.

"Yeah," Manuel agreed. "Good luck!" he added.

Without telling Mr. León about my conversation with Manuel, I approached him about our plans. "Mr. León, would it be okay with you if Manuel and I switch jobs again? I want a little more excitement and exercise. The pigs force me to spend too much time standing or sitting down. They rest too much. How about it? Can we do it?"

"Are you sure you want to do it? Have you forgotten the frightening night you spent up on a tree a long time ago and how the goats don't stop walking?" Mr. León asked.

"Yes, I do," I answered. "But that was a long time ago. I'm eleven years old now and I think I can handle it. I feel I can walk and run with the goats now that I am older," I added.

He must have seen my determination because he said, "Okay. I believe you can do it. I'll talk to Manuel. If he agrees, it will be okay with me. But remember. If you ever want to switch back, just let me know and we'll arrange the switch. But I don't think you will be asking for another switch. I'm sure you both want to keep your own herds."

The next afternoon, after Manuel and I put our herds away, Mr. León asked us to join him.

"Manuel," he said. "Julio wants to know if you are willing to swap jobs with him for a few days. What do you say?" As he saw us smiling at each other, Mr. León said, "Something tells me that you two have already decided. Am I right?"

"Yes, sir," answered Manuel. "I'm sorry, sir. I know it isn't up to us and we shouldn't have agreed to do it without first consulting with you. But we both think it's a good idea. But I guess you don't think so, right?"

"Hey, I trust both of you!" he answered. "I'm not opposed to the idea. I know you can do a good job with either herd. Go for it! But let me know whenever you want to end the switch, okay? Do you want to start tomorrow?" he inquired.

"Yes," we answered at the same time.

"Okay! Make sure you let your mothers know about the switch," he ordered.

The next day, we both picked up our new herds at sun up, as usual. Before we started out, Manuel and I met to wish each other good luck on our "new" jobs.

"Good luck, Julio," said Manuel. "Remember! Whenever either one of us wants to switch back, we have to let Mr. León know. But we have to discuss it ourselves first, okay?"

"Agreed, but let's hope it isn't too soon," I answered.

Nothing new happened in our routes for a while, except for the tired feeling I had every evening. I did make sure I would not lead the goats too close to the fence at the foot of the mountains. I did not want a repeat of what happened to me a year before. Soon, though, I had an incident that made me realize that I would have more trouble with the goats than I would have with the pigs.

The rainy season was in full swing. At this time, clouds usually appear in a few minutes and a downpour can come down all of a sudden.

One day, we were on our way back, still far away from the village, when lightning suddenly struck, followed by bursts of thunder. Needless to say, both the goats and I were startled and worried. I had been told to try to avoid getting caught out in the fields by a heavy storm but I wasn't told why.

When we were a few miles away from the village, the clouds got tired of holding their moisture and they let it all come down. It was a huge storm! Lightning and thunder had stopped but very heavy droplets were coming down. I was used to heavy storms but always in the safety of my house, never with a herd of goats, especially with little ones. I could tell they were scared so I tried to drive their fear away by talking to them. " Calm down, fellows. We'll be okay. Just hurry it up so we can get to the safety of our homes," I begged them.

Walking behind the herd, I soon noticed that a baby goat had fallen to the ground. I urged it to get up and to keep up with the rest of them. "Come on. Keep walking." When I noticed that it couldn't walk anymore, I picked it up saying, "Okay, I'll carry you for awhile. After resting for a while, you will be able to walk." Even though the rain had not let up, I put it down and ordered it to walk. It just couldn't. I had to pick it up again but, as I did, I saw another one on the ground.

"Oh, my God!" I screamed. "What will I do if another one falls? I have only two hands. Please, God, don't let others fall down. I can't carry any more. Oh, no, not another one! What will I do now? I'm sorry, little fellows, but I'll have to leave you behind. I'll come back to pick you up later. May God keep you safe!"

The storm continued and so did our walking. As we got closer to the village, two more fell down. Now there were five helpless ones. Even though I was afraid a coyote could find them and eat them, I took two in my arms and left three behind. "Mr. León will now think that switching jobs was a stupid idea," I thought.

For the second time in almost two years of working for Mr. León, I was afraid I would lose my job. Fortunately, we got home without losing another little one. I was hoping Mr. León would understand that I couldn't do anything but leave the kids behind. If someone had told me that this would happen during the rainy season, I wouldn't have come up with the stupid idea of switching jobs again. Now only God could help me keep my job.

By the time we arrived at Mr. León's house, the storm had stopped. I took the goats to their pen and I went to face him, expecting the worst.

"What happened? You couldn't make it home before the storm started? Did you lose any goats?" Mr. León asked.

"Five of the little ones dropped down. They simply couldn't walk anymore. I couldn't carry all five so I left three behind. I'm sorry, Mr. León. I never had this problem before. I'll go back for the other three. They are real close by," I explained.

"Wait a minute, Julio," he said. "Don't worry about it. This is a problem we always face during the rainy season. You're not the first one to feel helpless when the goats start dropping during a heavy storm. I'll send two other men to help you bring them back. Let's just hope they are all right."

After a few minutes, we returned with the three goats that had been overcome by the rain. They rejoined their mothers, who quickly and happily let their babies drink their milk. Soon, they looked as frisky as ever. Mr. León seemed happy, too.

CHAPTER 6

JULIO DECIDES TO STICK WITH PIG HERDING

That same evening, Manuel came to see me and we discussed another switch.

"Julio," he said. "I heard about the problem you had today. You know, that is nothing unusual. During the rainy season, when I had the goats, I often had the same problem and Mr. León understands that those things will happen. I wouldn't worry if I were you. But if you ever want to switch back, I'll be happy to do it. The pigs can get real mean. What do you say? Do you want them back?"

"Yeah. Let's switch back," I answered. "I think I'd rather put up with those mean males than with the little goats. We'll switch back tomorrow. But first, we have to let Mr. León know. Let's go see him now," I suggested.

"No! Let's do it tomorrow," Manuel objected. "I'm too tired and I want to go home," he added.

"Okay. But don't forget to be at his house earlier than normal so we can talk to him." I insisted.

Early the next morning, we knocked on his door and Mr. León came out.

"Good morning, boys," he greeted us. "What's up? How come you're here so early? Is something wrong or are you ready to call the switch off? After what happened to Julio yesterday, I was almost sure he would ask you to switch back, Manuel. Am I right? Don't feel bad if that's what you want, Julio. But I will tell you again. What happened to you is not unusual. Little goats just can't walk during a heavy downpour."

"Well, Mr. León, you're right. We did discuss it and we want to switch for good. Thank you for understanding. We want to start today. That's why we came here early," I stated.

"Okay, boys. It's getting a little late. Go to it," ordered Mr. León.

"We're going. Thanks!" we both hollered as we ran toward our respective pens.

I opened the pig's pen and led them out toward the nearest road. We followed it for a while. Soon, we set out for the harvested fields, where workers had left enough food behind for the pigs and for people eager to pick up a few food items. Corn and squash are the main crops grown in this area. There is plenty left over corn, still on the cob, considered not fit to be harvested. During the harvesting, these undesirables are trampled to the ground where pigs find them as full cobs of corn or as individual kernels. They had a ball finding them and eating them.

After a few hours, we left this area and walked on to another one. Again, the pigs gorged themselves on what they could find. Soon, though, the sun grew hot and the pigs got restless. I spotted a big, shady tree and we headed toward it. One by one, they started lying down and some even started snoring. This was the time for me to sit down at a distance and eat my lunch.

About an hour later, we set out again. We came to a road, crossed it and found ourselves at a new grazing area. The main crops grown here were watermelon and cantaloupe. It happened to be just north of an area flooded by heavy rains. The rain water had been there for some time, turning the area into a huge swamp. It was off limits to pig herders because pigs love water and mud and, if they see it, they will create problems for the pig herders. The pigs will rush to it and, once in it, it is hard to get them out. I took them to this area, even though I knew I could have problems.

Everything worked out smoothly for a while. But then, a man from my village named José Rodríguez came up to me and we started a conversation. We talked for so long that I forgot to keep my eyes on the pigs. By the time I remembered them, I saw that quite a few of them had wandered off toward the flooded area. Now I knew I was in real trouble. We both ran after them, trying to keep them from getting into the water. But it was too late. They got in and they soon were playing in the mud. (I suppose everybody knows that wallowing in the mud is a pig's main means of having fun.) The biggest ones went in deeper and were dipping their heads into the water, digging with their snouts, looking for whatever they could find.

Thinking that he was the cause of my problem, José went after the big pigs. The water was knee-deep but he rolled up his pants' legs up to his knees and waded in. He seemed to be quite agile running in the water, yelling, "Come on, you dirty, mud-sucking beasts! Get out of the water! It's getting late and you have to get home! Come on, come on!" He took his belt off and started whipping their behinds. It seemed to work with most of them but one of them turned around and tried to chase him. But José was a big guy and he did not seem to be afraid of it. He whipped his belt at the pig and it quickly turned around and joined the other pigs.

As he and the pigs came out of the water, he took me aside and said, "That swamp is full of those creatures. Look at my legs and tell me how many you can see."

"Six or seven, I think. I don't know. There may be more," I said. "What are they? Can you get them off? What will they do to you?" I inquired.

"They are called "leeches" and they suck your blood," he answered. "Have you ever had any of them stick to your body?" he asked me.

"No, never," I answered. "I hope I never get any of them on my skin," I added.

"But you went into the water, too. Let's find out. Do you feel any of them clinging to your skin? Let's see. Raise up your pants' legs," he ordered.

"Okay, but I don't feel any . . . . .Yuck!" I shuddered, grimacing when I noticed three sticking to my ankle. "How do you take them off? Hurry, hurry! Take them off!" I begged him.

"Of course, you don't feel them. But don't worry. They won't kill you. I'll take mine off with a cigarette and yours with soap. I usually carry some soap in my backpack to wash my hands. Here it is! Come closer. I'll rub yours off with this soap," he said.

He rubbed mine off in no time. Then, he lit a cigarette and burned his off.

In the meantime, the pigs were huddling together, grunting and squealing. They must have been laughing at us. They had some leeches on their bodies but they seemed to come off readily as they moved around.

Before José said good-bye, he apologized. "I'm sorry for the trouble I caused you. If I hadn't stopped to chat with you we wouldn't have had to get in the water and have those leeches hook on to our skin. But everything turned out okay, right?" he asked.

"Right," I agreed. "But don't apologize. It was more my fault. Actually, you taught me a valuable lesson about leeches. I didn't know anything about them.

Now, if I ever have to get into swampy water and they stick to me, I won't be too afraid of them. Thanks, José, and see you some other time. Bye, bye."

As soon as José took off, I rounded up my pigs and started back home. When we got there, Mr. León came out of his house and asked, "How was your day, Julio? Did you meet anybody out in the fields?"

"Well, yes, sir, I did," I answered. "Mr. José Rodríguez stopped by to chat with me for a while and, while we talked, my pigs wandered into a swampy area full of leeches. I was scared, I'm ashamed to admit, but . . . ."

"I know. José told me all about it," he interrupted. "He also said you acted quite grownup when you told him that the incident was more your fault than his. That speaks very well of you, Julio. I'm proud of you. Try to avoid that area next time so you won't have any more problems with leeches. You don't want them to suck your blood, do you? " he asked.

"They won't do that, will they? That would kill me, right?" I asked.

"No, no! They won't do that. You can always take them off," he assured me.

"Mr. León, just to make sure my blood is safe, I'll make sure the pigs won't get near that swampy area. You can bet on that! See you tomorrow," I said.

"Good! See you tomorrow, Julio," he said.

That night, after a supper that consisted of corn tortillas and a bowl of boiled beans with hot sauce, we gathered around my mother, who had something to tell us.

"Listen, children. We simply cannot go on like this. Four of us are working now and we still eat very poorly. There's a family of three who go to the United States every year and come back home with lots of money after working up there for a few months. I think we'll join them when they go back up north. They assured me that we would earn much more over there in one day than what we earn here in a week. I will have to borrow the money for the train fare," she said.

"Are we all going to the United States, mother?" I asked her eagerly.

"I hope so. But I don't know right now. If I can borrow enough money, we will all go. I would hate to leave any of you behind. It would be better if we stick together. We'll see, Julio," she answered.

CHAPTER 7

JULIO SAYS GOOD-BYE

After Mother gave us the news, I went to say good-bye to Mr. León and to Manuel. When I got to Mr. León's house, I knocked on the door and he came out right away. "Julio!" he exclaimed with a surprised look on his face. "What are you doing here at this time?" he asked.

"My mother just told us that we are going to the United States and we all have to go to San Antonio tomorrow," I answered. Then I added, "You were good enough to give me my first job and I felt I had to, at least, thank you and say good-bye to you. I'm sorry I was unable to give you the news earlier. In spite of the few problems I had herding your pigs and goats, I enjoyed my job and I want to thank you for trusting me with your animals. Thank you very, very much, Mr. León."

"You are very welcome, Julio. I was happy to be of help to you and your family. I wish you all the best of luck. If you do go to the United States, I wish you lots of luck in your schooling. I am almost sure you will be attending school over there because I was told that children are not allowed to work during the school year until they are sixteen years old," he assured me. "And if you don't go, you can always get a job with me," he added.

"Are you sure children have to go to school until they are sixteen years old? What if their parents want them to quit school so they can work?" I asked Mr. León.

"I don't know for sure but that is what people have told me," he answered . "You've grown quite a bit here but you're still only twelve years old. Wouldn't you like to go back to school?" he asked.

"I sure would! I would like to finish school so that I can get a better job. Who wouldn't?" I answered. "But if I can't go to school, I'm willing to work on anything I can do to help my family," I added.

"You have become a good little man, Julio," he said. "But remember, if you get a chance to go to school, take advantage of the opportunity. Perhaps you can become a teacher, a doctor or a lawyer. Good luck!" he added.

"I will take advantage of the opportunity," I promised. "Thank you very much, Mr. León. Good-bye," I said.

When I got to Manuel's house, he was outside playing with his dog. He, too, was surprised to see me.

"What are you doing here at this time, Julio? Is anything wrong?" he asked.

"No. Everything is okay," I answered. "I just came to say good-bye to you," I added.

"Why?" he inquired puzzled. "Where are you going?" he asked.

"My mother just told us that we are going to the United States and we have to go to San Antonio before our trip up north. I did not want to go without saying good-bye to you. But, unless we go up north right away, I will come visit you a few times," I promised.

"Yes, I'm sure you will visit your village once in a while. Look me up when you do, okay?" he begged.

“I sure will,” I promised. “Well, I guess I have to go. We’re leaving for San Antonio real early in the morning tomorrow so I’d better go. Good-bye. Take care of yourself and your herd,” I ordered.

“I sure will,” he promised.

“Take care of yourself too, okay? I hope we will see each other soon. Good-bye,” he added.

As I was walking back home, the idea of going to the United States excited me a lot. Even though I still did not know if I was going, a few questions invaded my mind: "If I do go to the United States, what will the trip be like? What will I be doing once we get there? Will I be going to school as Mr. León said or will I spend the rest of my life working out in the fields? And if I do go to school, will I be able to become somebody important, other than a mere field worker?"

But then I realized that I didn't speak that country's language. And as much as I tried to get those questions out of my mind, I just couldn't. They kept going in and out of my head. But of one thing I was sure. The language will be an obstacle at first but I'm sure I will be able to learn it. By God! I can do it!